Oracle Essential Bible

A Comprehensive A-Z Guide for Absolute Beginner

Max G. Ardenvil

TABLE OF CONTENTS

Introduction to Oracle Database..12
What is Oracle?..12
History and Evolution of Oracle...13
Key Milestones in Oracle's Evolution...13
Key Features and Benefits of Oracle Database...15
Key Features..15
Benefits of Using Oracle..16
Understanding Relational Database Management Systems (RDBMS)...........16
Oracle Editions and Versions...17
Getting Started with Oracle..18
Installing Oracle Database...18
System Requirements...18
Downloading Oracle Database..18
Installing Oracle on Windows...19
Installing Oracle on Linux...19
Oracle Database Architecture Overview..20
1. Physical Components...20
2. Memory Structures..20
3. Process Structures..20
Oracle Client vs. Server...21
Oracle Server...21
Oracle Client..21
Oracle SQL Developer and Other Tools..21
Oracle SQL Developer..21
Installing SQL Developer...21
Connecting to an Oracle Database in SQL Developer...........................22
Other Oracle Database Tools..22
Creating Your First Database..22
Using DBCA (Database Configuration Assistant)......................................22
Creating a Database Manually..23
SQL Fundamentals in Oracle...24
Introduction to Structured Query Language (SQL)..24
SQL Categories..24
Writing Basic SQL Queries...25

Example: Retrieving All Data from a Table..25

Retrieving Specific Columns..26

Using SELECT, FROM, WHERE Clauses..26

1. SELECT Clause..26

2. FROM Clause..26

3. WHERE Clause...26

Comparison Operators in WHERE Clause..27

Example: Fetching Employees with High Salary....................................27

Sorting and Filtering Data..27

ORDER BY Clause...27

Filtering Data Using Logical Operators...28

1. AND Operator (Both conditions must be true)....................................28

2. OR Operator (Either condition must be true).....................................28

3. IN Operator (Matches values in a list)...28

4. BETWEEN Operator (Checks range of values)..................................28

5. LIKE Operator (Pattern matching using wildcards)...........................29

Aggregate Functions and Grouping...29

Aggregate Functions in Oracle SQL...29

Examples of Aggregate Functions..30

Counting Employees..30

Calculating Total Salaries..30

Finding Maximum and Minimum Salary...30

Grouping Data Using GROUP BY...30

Example: Total Salaries by Department..30

Using GROUP BY with COUNT()...31

Filtering Grouped Data Using HAVING Clause..31

Example: Departments with Total Salaries Above 50,000......................31

Working with Tables and Data Manipulation in Oracle................................32

Creating and Managing Tables...32

Understanding Tables in Oracle..32

Creating a Table..32

Syntax..32

Example: Creating an Employees Table...33

Altering a Table...33

Adding a New Column..33

Modifying a Column Data Type..33

Dropping a Column...34

Dropping a Table...34

Data Types in Oracle..34

Common Data Types...34

INSERT, UPDATE, DELETE Statements...35

Inserting Data into a Table...35

    Inserting a Single Row..35

    Inserting Multiple Rows...35

Updating Data in a Table...36

    Updating a Single Column..36

    Updating Multiple Columns..36

Deleting Data from a Table...36

    Deleting a Single Record..36

    Deleting Multiple Records...37

    Deleting All Data (Truncate vs. Delete)..37

Constraints and Indexes...37

Constraints in Oracle...37

    Types of Constraints...37

Indexes in Oracle..38

    Creating an Index...38

    Creating a Unique Index..38

    Dropping an Index..39

Managing Large Data Sets..39

Partitioning Tables...39

    Example: Range Partitioning..39

Bulk Data Processing...40

    Using Bulk Inserts..40

    Using Bulk Collect for Fetching Large Data..40

Archiving Old Data..41

Oracle Database Objects..**42**

Understanding Views and Materialized Views...42

What is a View?..42

Creating a View..42

    Example: Creating a View..42

Using a View..43

Updating a View..43

Dropping a View...43

Materialized Views..43

Creating a Materialized View..43

Refreshing a Materialized View...44

Dropping a Materialized View...44

Using Sequences and Synonyms...44

Sequences...44

Creating a Sequence...44

Using a Sequence in an INSERT Statement..45

Dropping a Sequence..45

Synonyms...45

Creating a Synonym...45

Dropping a Synonym..46

Working with Stored Procedures and Functions...46

Stored Procedures...46

Creating a Stored Procedure..46

Executing a Stored Procedure..46

Dropping a Stored Procedure...47

Functions..47

Creating a Function...47

Using a Function...47

Dropping a Function..48

Triggers and Their Uses..48

Types of Triggers..48

Creating a Trigger...48

Dropping a Trigger..49

Introduction to Packages...49

Advantages of Packages..49

Creating a Package Specification..49

Creating a Package Body..50

Using the Package...51

Dropping a Package...51

PL/SQL Programming for Beginners...52

What is PL/SQL?...52

Why Use PL/SQL?...52

PL/SQL Program Structure...52

Example of a Basic PL/SQL Block...53

Variables, Data Types, and Control Structures..53

Declaring Variables...53

Syntax...53

Example..53

Data Types in PL/SQL...54

Control Structures...55

Conditional Statements...55

Loops in PL/SQL...55

Cursors and Exception Handling..57

Cursors in PL/SQL..57

Implicit Cursor (Automatic)..57

Explicit Cursor (Manual Control)..58

Exception Handling...59

Predefined Exceptions..59

Example..59
Creating and Using PL/SQL Procedures...60
Creating a Stored Procedure...60
Executing a Procedure...61
Dropping a Procedure..61
PL/SQL Best Practices...61
User Management and Security..**62**
Creating and Managing Users..62
Creating a User in Oracle...62
Syntax:..62
Example:...63
Assigning Default Tablespace and Quotas..63
Altering a User...63
Dropping a User...64
Granting and Revoking Privileges...64
Granting Privileges..64
Granting System Privileges...64
Granting Object Privileges...65
Revoking Privileges...65
Roles and Profiles...65
Roles in Oracle..65
Creating a Role...65
Assigning Privileges to a Role...66
Assigning a Role to a User...66
Revoking a Role...66
Profiles in Oracle...66
Creating a Profile...66
Assigning a Profile to a User...67
Implementing Security Best Practices...67
Auditing and Monitoring User Activity...67
Enabling Standard Auditing...67
Viewing Audit Logs..68
Using Fine-Grained Auditing (FGA)...68
Creating an FGA Policy..68
Monitoring Active Sessions..69
Oracle Backup and Recovery...**70**
Understanding Backup and Recovery Concepts..70
What is Backup?...70
What is Recovery?..70
Types of Oracle Backups..71
1. Physical vs. Logical Backups...71

2. Full vs. Incremental Backups...71

3. Cold (Offline) vs. Hot (Online) Backups...71

4. Archive Log Backups...71

Choosing the Right Backup Type...72

Using Recovery Manager (RMAN)..72

What is RMAN?...72

Setting Up RMAN..72

Performing Incremental Backups..73

Performing Data Recovery..73

1. Restoring a Full Database..73

2. Recovering a Tablespace..74

3. Recovering a Datafile..74

4. Performing Point-in-Time Recovery (PITR)..74

5. Recovering from Archived Logs..75

Best Practices for Data Protection..75

1. Enable ARCHIVELOG Mode..75

2. Schedule Regular Backups...75

3. Store Backups in Multiple Locations..75

4. Test Backup and Recovery Procedures...76

5. Implement Data Encryption...76

6. Monitor Backup Performance...76

7. Use Flashback Technologies..76

Oracle Performance Tuning Basics...**77**

Understanding Database Performance Issues...77

What is Performance Tuning?..77

Common Database Performance Issues..77

Key Metrics for Performance Monitoring..78

Optimizing SQL Queries...79

1. Writing Efficient SQL Queries..79

Use SELECT Only What You Need...79

Use EXISTS Instead of IN for Subqueries...80

Use Joins Instead of Subqueries..80

Use Bind Variables...81

Using EXPLAIN PLAN and Indexing..81

1. Using EXPLAIN PLAN..81

Generating an Execution Plan...81

Interpreting the Execution Plan...82

2. Using Indexing for Performance Improvement..82

Types of Indexes..82

Creating an Index...83

Using Function-Based Index...83

Checking Index Usage...83

Monitoring System Performance..83

    1. Using V$ Views for Performance Analysis.................................84

        Checking Active Sessions..84

        Identifying Slow Queries..84

        Checking Wait Events...84

Basic Troubleshooting Techniques..85

    1. Identify High CPU Usage Queries...85

    2. Fix Full Table Scans..85

    3. Analyze Locking Issues..85

    4. Tune Database Memory...85

    5. Rebuild Indexes if Fragmented..85

Working with Oracle Cloud Database..**86**

Introduction to Oracle Cloud Infrastructure (OCI).............................86

    Key Features of Oracle Cloud Infrastructure...............................86

    Oracle Database Deployment Options in OCI.............................87

Deploying and Managing Oracle Databases in the Cloud..................87

    Steps to Deploy an Oracle Database in OCI...............................88

    Managing Oracle Cloud Databases...88

Cloud Security and Best Practices..89

    Key Security Features in OCI..89

    Best Practices for Cloud Security...89

Backup and Disaster Recovery in the Cloud.......................................90

    Types of Backups in Oracle Cloud...90

    Configuring Automatic Backups..90

    Disaster Recovery Solutions...91

Oracle Autonomous Database...91

    Key Features of Oracle Autonomous Database............................91

    Types of Autonomous Databases...91

    Deploying an Autonomous Database..92

    Managing an Autonomous Database..92

Real-World Applications of Oracle...**93**

Using Oracle in Enterprise Applications..93

    Key Features of Oracle for Enterprises..93

    Common Enterprise Use Cases..94

Oracle for Business Intelligence and Data Warehousing...................95

    What is Business Intelligence (BI)?..95

    Oracle Data Warehousing Solutions..95

    Business Intelligence Workflow with Oracle.................................95

    Industries Using Oracle for BI...95

Oracle and Big Data Integration..96

How Oracle Integrates with Big Data..96

Oracle Technologies for Big Data..97

Big Data Use Cases with Oracle...97

Case Studies and Industry Examples..98

1. Banking and Finance – JPMorgan Chase..98

2. Retail – Walmart...98

3. Healthcare – Mayo Clinic...98

4. Telecommunications – AT&T...98

Learning Paths for Oracle Certification...98

Popular Oracle Certifications...99

Steps to Get Certified...99

Resources and Next Steps...100

Recommended Books and Online Courses...100

Books for Further Learning..100

Online Courses and Training..101

Oracle Certification Paths...102

Popular Oracle Certifications and Paths...102

Steps to Get Certified...103

Oracle Community and Support Forums..104

Official Oracle Communities..104

Popular Online Forums and Groups...104

Oracle Conferences and Events...104

Keeping Up with Oracle Updates..105

Ways to Stay Updated...105

Final Thoughts and Best Practices...105

1. Build a Strong Foundation...105

2. Practice with Real-World Scenarios...105

3. Follow Security Best Practices...106

4. Optimize for Performance..106

5. Stay Curious and Keep Learning...106

What's Next?...106

Glossary of Terms..108

A...108

B...108

C...109

D...109

E...110

F...110

G..111

H..111

I..111

J.. 112

K.. 112

L.. 112

M.. 112

N.. 112

O.. 113

P.. 113

R.. 113

S-Z.. 113

Introduction to Oracle Database

Oracle Database is one of the most widely used and powerful relational database management systems (RDBMS) in the world. It provides robust data storage, retrieval, and management capabilities for businesses, government institutions, and individuals. Designed for high performance, scalability, and security, Oracle Database is a preferred choice for enterprises handling vast amounts of structured data.

What is Oracle?

Oracle is a database management system developed by Oracle Corporation that allows users to store, retrieve, and manage data efficiently. It is a **relational database management system (RDBMS)**, meaning it organizes data in tables with predefined relationships. Oracle Database is known for its ability to handle large-scale data workloads, complex queries, and high transaction volumes.

Oracle is designed to support:

- **Online Transaction Processing (OLTP)** – Handling large numbers of transactions in real-time.
- **Online Analytical Processing (OLAP)** – Processing complex queries for business intelligence and data analysis.
- **Hybrid Workloads** – A combination of OLTP and OLAP workloads to support modern data-driven applications.

With built-in tools for security, backup, disaster recovery, and performance tuning, Oracle is used in industries such as finance, healthcare, telecommunications, and e-commerce.

History and Evolution of Oracle

Oracle Corporation was founded in 1977 by **Larry Ellison, Bob Miner, and Ed Oates** under the name Software Development Laboratories (SDL). Their vision was to create a powerful, flexible, and scalable database system based on relational database theory.

Key Milestones in Oracle's Evolution

1. **Oracle Version 1 (1978-1979)**

   - The first version was written in assembly language for the PDP-11 minicomputer.
   - It was never officially released but set the foundation for future versions.

2. **Oracle Version 2 (1979-1983)**

   - The first commercial version released in 1979.
   - Introduced basic SQL support, making Oracle one of the earliest commercial SQL-based databases.

3. **Oracle Version 3 (1983-1985)**

   - First version written in C, making it portable across different operating systems.
   - Introduced transaction processing and concurrency control.

4. **Oracle Version 4 (1985-1988)**

   - Introduced **read consistency**, an important feature in database management.
   - Added basic recovery mechanisms.

5. **Oracle Version 5 (1988-1990)**

   o First version with client-server architecture support.
   o Introduced **Oracle Networking**, enabling remote database access.

6. **Oracle Version 6 (1990-1992)**

   o Introduced **PL/SQL**, Oracle's proprietary procedural language.
   o Added **row-level locking**, improving concurrency.

7. **Oracle7 (1992-1997)**

   o Introduced stored procedures, triggers, and improved scalability.
   o First version to be widely adopted by enterprises.

8. **Oracle8 and Oracle8i (1997-2001)**

   o Support for **object-oriented features** and **multimedia data types**.
   o Introduction of **Internet computing features** with Oracle8i, enabling web-based applications.

9. **Oracle9i (2001-2003)**

   o Introduced **Real Application Clusters (RAC)** for high availability.
   o Introduced **Data Guard** for disaster recovery.

10. **Oracle10g (2003-2007)**

    o Introduced **grid computing**, improving scalability and flexibility.
    o Enhanced performance tuning and self-management capabilities.

11. **Oracle11g (2007-2013)**

    o Introduced **automatic memory management** and advanced compression.
    o Improved **PL/SQL performance** and **SQL Result Cache**.

12. **Oracle12c (2013-2018)**

    o First version with **multi-tenant architecture**, enabling cloud computing.
    o Improved **partitioning and in-memory database** capabilities.

13. **Oracle18c (2018-2019)**

   ○ First database to introduce **autonomous features**, automating tasks like tuning, backups, and security.

14. **Oracle19c (2019-2021)**

   ○ Long-term support release with high performance and stability.
   ○ Enhanced machine learning and blockchain support.

15. **Oracle21c (2021-Present)**

   ○ Introduced **Blockchain Tables**, JSON enhancements, and AI/ML integration.
   ○ Supports new data types and cloud-native architectures.

16. **Oracle Cloud and Autonomous Database**

   ○ Oracle now focuses heavily on **cloud-based databases**, offering **Oracle Cloud Infrastructure (OCI)** and **Autonomous Database** solutions.

Key Features and Benefits of Oracle Database

Key Features

1. **Multi-Tenant Architecture** – Allows multiple databases to run in a single instance, improving efficiency.
2. **High Availability (HA) and Disaster Recovery (DR)** – Features like Real Application Clusters (RAC) and Data Guard ensure uptime.
3. **Advanced Security** – Offers encryption, user authentication, auditing, and fine-grained access control.
4. **Performance Optimization** – Uses indexing, in-memory computing, and caching to enhance performance.
5. **Scalability and Flexibility** – Supports both small applications and enterprise-scale data warehouses.

6. **PL/SQL Programming Language** – Allows developers to write stored procedures, triggers, and functions within the database.
7. **Automation and AI Integration** – Autonomous database management reduces manual tuning and maintenance.
8. **Cloud Integration** – Fully compatible with Oracle Cloud and hybrid cloud solutions.

Benefits of Using Oracle

- **Reliability** – Designed for mission-critical applications with minimal downtime.
- **Security** – Protects sensitive data with robust security protocols.
- **Scalability** – Adapts to growing business needs without performance degradation.
- **Compliance** – Supports compliance standards such as GDPR, HIPAA, and PCI DSS.
- **Innovation** – Continuous improvements with AI, blockchain, and cloud-based solutions.

Understanding Relational Database Management Systems (RDBMS)

A **Relational Database Management System (RDBMS)** organizes data in tables and establishes relationships between them. Oracle follows the relational model, where:

- **Data is stored in tables (relations).**
- **Each table consists of rows (records) and columns (attributes).**
- **Tables are linked using primary and foreign keys.**
- **SQL (Structured Query Language) is used to interact with the database.**

Oracle implements advanced RDBMS features such as:

- **ACID Compliance (Atomicity, Consistency, Isolation, Durability)**
- **Normalization to reduce data redundancy**
- **Concurrency control mechanisms**

Oracle Editions and Versions

Oracle offers different **editions** based on business needs:

1. **Oracle Database Standard Edition (SE2)**

   ○ Ideal for small to medium businesses.
   ○ Supports basic enterprise features but lacks advanced clustering and automation.

2. **Oracle Database Enterprise Edition (EE)**

   ○ Suitable for large enterprises with high transaction volumes.
   ○ Includes advanced security, performance tuning, and disaster recovery features.

3. **Oracle Express Edition (XE)**

   ○ A free, lightweight version for small applications and learning purposes.
   ○ Limited storage, CPU, and memory.

4. **Oracle Cloud Database**

   ○ Fully managed cloud-based database.
   ○ Includes **Autonomous Database**, which automates security, tuning, and scaling.

5. **Oracle Personal Edition**

   ○ Designed for single-user development and testing.
   ○ Supports all features of Enterprise Edition but lacks RAC support.

Oracle Database remains a dominant force in the database world due to its scalability, reliability, and continuous innovation. Beginners who learn Oracle can build skills that are highly valued in enterprise IT environments.

Getting Started with Oracle

Oracle Database is a powerful and sophisticated relational database management system (RDBMS) used in various industries. Before diving into SQL and database management, it is essential to understand how to set up Oracle, its architecture, and the tools available for interacting with the database.

Installing Oracle Database

Installing Oracle Database is the first step to working with it. Oracle provides multiple installation options depending on the operating system and version.

System Requirements

Before installation, ensure your system meets the following minimum requirements:

- **Operating System:** Windows 10/11, macOS (for client tools), or Linux
- **RAM:** At least 8GB (Recommended: 16GB for better performance)
- **Storage:** At least 20GB free disk space
- **Processor:** Intel or AMD with at least 2 cores
- **User Privileges:** Administrative access for installation

Downloading Oracle Database

Oracle provides different editions of its database software, including:

1. **Oracle Database Express Edition (XE) – Free and lightweight**
2. **Oracle Database Standard Edition – Suitable for small businesses**
3. **Oracle Database Enterprise Edition – Full-featured for large enterprises**

4. **Oracle Autonomous Database – Fully managed cloud-based option**

To download Oracle Database:

1. Visit Oracle's official website
2. Choose the appropriate edition (XE is recommended for beginners)
3. Download the installer for your operating system
4. Accept the Oracle license agreement

Installing Oracle on Windows

1. **Run the Installer** – Double-click the downloaded file and follow the setup wizard.
2. **Choose Installation Type** – Select **Server Class** (for advanced configurations) or **Desktop Class** (for basic setup).
3. **Set Configuration Options** – Define a database name, password, and storage location.
4. **Create an Oracle Home User** – Choose an existing Windows user or create a new one.
5. **Finalize Installation** – The setup will install Oracle Database and services.

Verify Installation – Open a command prompt and enter:
sqlplus / as sysdba

6. If SQL*Plus opens without errors, the installation was successful.

Installing Oracle on Linux

1. Download the RPM or ZIP file from Oracle's website.

Extract or install it using:
rpm -ivh oracle-database-ee-19c-1.0-1.x86_64.rpm

2. Configure the database:
   /etc/init.d/oracle-xe configure
3. Start the database service:
   systemctl start oracle-xe
4. Verify installation with SQL*Plus.

Oracle Database Architecture Overview

Oracle Database has a well-structured architecture that consists of physical and logical components to manage data efficiently.

1. Physical Components

- **Data Files** – Store actual database data.
- **Control Files** – Maintain database metadata, structure, and status.
- **Redo Log Files** – Record all changes for recovery purposes.
- **Archived Logs** – Backup copies of redo logs for recovery.

2. Memory Structures

- **System Global Area (SGA)** – Shared memory for caching data and SQL execution.
- **Program Global Area (PGA)** – Memory allocated per user session for sorting and buffering.
- **Shared Pool** – Stores SQL statements and execution plans.
- **Buffer Cache** – Holds frequently accessed database blocks.
- **Redo Log Buffer** – Stores transaction logs before writing to disk.

3. Process Structures

- **Background Processes** – Oracle runs multiple processes like **DBWR (Database Writer), LGWR (Log Writer), CKPT (Checkpoint), and SMON (System Monitor)**.
- **User Processes** – Created for each database session.
- **Server Processes** – Handle user requests and execute SQL statements.

Understanding these components helps optimize database performance and troubleshoot issues.

Oracle Client vs. Server

Oracle follows a **client-server architecture**, allowing multiple users to access a database over a network.

Oracle Server

- The Oracle **Server** hosts the database instance and manages storage, transactions, and user access.
- It runs on **dedicated servers** or cloud environments.
- Components include **Oracle Instance (SGA + background processes)** and **Physical Database (data files, control files, redo logs)**.

Oracle Client

- The **Client** is an application that connects to the Oracle Server to query and manipulate data.
- Clients use **Oracle Net Services (TNS)** to communicate with the server.
- Common client tools: **SQL*Plus, SQL Developer, Toad, and JDBC/ODBC applications**.

Clients can be installed on user machines or web-based applications accessing the database remotely.

Oracle SQL Developer and Other Tools

Oracle SQL Developer

Oracle SQL Developer is a **free integrated development environment (IDE)** for managing Oracle databases. It provides:

- A graphical user interface (GUI) for running SQL queries.
- Database administration tools.
- Support for PL/SQL development.

Installing SQL Developer

1. Download SQL Developer from Oracle's website.
2. Extract and install the software (Java is required).
3. Launch SQL Developer and configure a connection.

Connecting to an Oracle Database in SQL Developer

1. Open SQL Developer.
2. Click **New Connection**.
3. Enter:
   - **Username:** system
   - **Password:** (set during installation)
   - **Hostname:** localhost (or server IP)
   - **Port:** 1521
   - **Service Name:** orcl (default name)
4. Click **Test Connection**, then **Connect**.

Other Oracle Database Tools

- **SQL*Plus** – A command-line tool for executing SQL queries.
- **Oracle Enterprise Manager (OEM)** – A web-based administration tool for monitoring databases.
- **Toad for Oracle** – A popular third-party database development tool.
- **Oracle Cloud Console** – For managing cloud-based Oracle databases.

Creating Your First Database

Once Oracle is installed, you can create a new database instance.

Using DBCA (Database Configuration Assistant)

1. Open **DBCA** from the Oracle menu.
2. Select **Create a New Database**.
3. Choose **Advanced Mode** (for custom settings) or **Typical Mode** (for default settings).
4. Set the **Global Database Name** (e.g., orcl).

5. Define administrative credentials.
6. Configure **Memory Allocation**, **Storage**, and **Redo Log Settings**.
7. Click **Finish** to create the database.

Creating a Database Manually

For advanced users, Oracle allows manual database creation using SQL commands.

Start the Database Instance:
 STARTUP NOMOUNT;

1. **Create the Database**:
    CREATE DATABASE orcl

USER SYS IDENTIFIED BY admin

USER SYSTEM IDENTIFIED BY admin

LOGFILE GROUP 1 ('/u01/app/oracle/oradata/orcl/redo01.log') SIZE 50M,

   GROUP 2 ('/u01/app/oracle/oradata/orcl/redo02.log') SIZE 50M

MAXLOGFILES 5

MAXDATAFILES 100

CHARACTER SET AL32UTF8;

2. **Run Catalog and Data Dictionary Scripts**:
    @?/rdbms/admin/catalog.sql

@?/rdbms/admin/catproc.sql

3. **Open the Database**:
    ALTER DATABASE OPEN;

Once the database is created, you can start writing SQL queries to store and retrieve data.

SQL Fundamentals in Oracle

Structured Query Language (SQL) is the backbone of all relational database management systems, including Oracle. It is used for storing, manipulating, and retrieving data efficiently. Oracle SQL follows the ANSI SQL standard while also providing proprietary extensions for enhanced functionality.

This chapter will cover the fundamental SQL concepts needed to interact with an Oracle database, including writing queries, using clauses, sorting and filtering data, and performing aggregate operations.

Introduction to Structured Query Language (SQL)

SQL is a standardized language used to manage data in relational database management systems (RDBMS). Oracle SQL enables users to perform operations such as:

- Creating and modifying database objects (tables, views, indexes).
- Inserting, updating, deleting, and retrieving data.
- Controlling user access to data.
- Managing database transactions.

SQL Categories

SQL is divided into several subcategories based on its functionalities:

1. **Data Query Language (DQL)** – Used to retrieve data.

   o SELECT

2. **Data Definition Language (DDL)** – Used to define and modify database structures.

   o CREATE, ALTER, DROP, TRUNCATE
3. **Data Manipulation Language (DML)** – Used to manipulate data within tables.

   o INSERT, UPDATE, DELETE, MERGE
4. **Data Control Language (DCL)** – Used to manage access privileges.

   o GRANT, REVOKE
5. **Transaction Control Language (TCL)** – Used to manage database transactions.

   o COMMIT, ROLLBACK, SAVEPOINT

Understanding these categories helps in effectively managing an Oracle database.

Writing Basic SQL Queries

A basic SQL query retrieves data from a database using the SELECT statement. The general syntax is:

SELECT column1, column2, ...

FROM table_name

WHERE condition;

Example: Retrieving All Data from a Table

SELECT * FROM employees;

This query selects all columns from the employees table.

Retrieving Specific Columns

SELECT first_name, last_name, salary FROM employees;

Only first_name, last_name, and salary are retrieved.

Using SELECT, FROM, WHERE Clauses

1. SELECT Clause

The SELECT statement is used to retrieve data from tables.

SELECT first_name, department_id FROM employees;

This retrieves first_name and department_id from the employees table.

2. FROM Clause

Specifies the table from which data is retrieved. Multiple tables can be specified in **JOIN** queries.

SELECT * FROM departments;

This selects all columns from the departments table.

3. WHERE Clause

Filters records based on a condition.

SELECT first_name, last_name FROM employees

WHERE department_id = 10;

This retrieves employees only from department **10**.

Comparison Operators in WHERE Clause

- = Equal to
- != or <> Not equal to
- > Greater than
- < Less than
- >= Greater than or equal to
- <= Less than or equal to

Example: Fetching Employees with High Salary

SELECT first_name, last_name, salary FROM employees

WHERE salary > 5000;

Retrieves employees earning more than **5000**.

Sorting and Filtering Data

ORDER BY Clause

Used to **sort** query results in ascending (ASC) or descending (DESC) order.

SELECT first_name, salary FROM employees

ORDER BY salary DESC;

Sorts employees in descending order of salary.

Filtering Data Using Logical Operators

1. AND Operator (Both conditions must be true)

SELECT * FROM employees

WHERE salary > 5000 AND department_id = 20;

Retrieves employees with **salary > 5000** and in **department 20**.

2. OR Operator (Either condition must be true)

SELECT * FROM employees

WHERE job_id = 'IT_PROG' OR job_id = 'HR_REP';

Fetches employees working as either **IT_PROG** or **HR_REP**.

3. IN Operator (Matches values in a list)

SELECT * FROM employees

WHERE department_id IN (10, 20, 30);

Retrieves employees in departments **10, 20, or 30**.

4. BETWEEN Operator (Checks range of values)

SELECT * FROM employees

WHERE salary BETWEEN 3000 AND 7000;

Fetches employees with salaries between **3000** and **7000**.

5. LIKE Operator (Pattern matching using wildcards)

- % – Matches multiple characters.
- _ – Matches a single character.

Example: Find employees whose names start with 'A':

SELECT * FROM employees

WHERE first_name LIKE 'A%';

Finds names such as **Alice, Andrew, Amanda**.

Aggregate Functions and Grouping

Aggregate Functions in Oracle SQL

Aggregate functions perform calculations on multiple rows and return a **single** value.

Function	Description	Example
COUNT()	Counts number of records	COUNT(*)
SUM()	Calculates total sum	SUM(salary)
AVG()	Computes average	AVG(salary)

| MAX() | Returns maximum value | MAX(salary) |
| MIN() | Returns minimum value | MIN(salary) |

Examples of Aggregate Functions

Counting Employees

SELECT COUNT(*) FROM employees;

Returns total number of employees.

Calculating Total Salaries

SELECT SUM(salary) FROM employees;

Returns the total sum of salaries.

Finding Maximum and Minimum Salary

SELECT MAX(salary), MIN(salary) FROM employees;

Retrieves highest and lowest salary values.

Grouping Data Using GROUP BY

The GROUP BY clause is used to group rows with the same values in specified columns.

Example: Total Salaries by Department

SELECT department_id, SUM(salary)

FROM employees

GROUP BY department_id;

Groups employees by department and calculates total salary per department.

Using GROUP BY with COUNT()

SELECT job_id, COUNT(*) AS employee_count

FROM employees

GROUP BY job_id;

Counts the number of employees in each job role.

Filtering Grouped Data Using HAVING Clause

The HAVING clause filters groups based on aggregate results (unlike WHERE, which filters individual rows).

Example: Departments with Total Salaries Above 50,000

SELECT department_id, SUM(salary)

FROM employees

GROUP BY department_id

HAVING SUM(salary) > 50000;

Displays only departments where the **total salary exceeds 50,000**.

Working with Tables and Data Manipulation in Oracle

Oracle Database provides powerful tools for creating and managing tables, inserting and modifying data, enforcing data integrity, and optimizing performance using indexes. This chapter will explore how to create and manage tables, understand data types, perform data manipulation operations, enforce constraints, and efficiently handle large datasets.

Creating and Managing Tables

Understanding Tables in Oracle

A table in Oracle is a collection of related data stored in rows and columns. Each row represents a record, while each column represents an attribute of the data.

Creating a Table

The CREATE TABLE statement is used to define a new table with specified columns and data types.

Syntax

CREATE TABLE table_name (

    column1 datatype constraint,

    column2 datatype constraint,

    ...

```
);
```

Example: Creating an Employees Table

```
CREATE TABLE employees (

    employee_id NUMBER(10) PRIMARY KEY,

    first_name VARCHAR2(50),

    last_name VARCHAR2(50) NOT NULL,

    email VARCHAR2(100) UNIQUE,

    hire_date DATE DEFAULT SYSDATE,

    salary NUMBER(10,2) CHECK (salary > 0),

    department_id NUMBER(10),

    CONSTRAINT fk_department FOREIGN KEY (department_id)
REFERENCES departments(department_id)

);
```

Altering a Table

The ALTER TABLE statement is used to modify an existing table structure.

Adding a New Column

```
ALTER TABLE employees ADD phone_number VARCHAR2(15);
```

Modifying a Column Data Type

```
ALTER TABLE employees MODIFY salary NUMBER(12,2);
```

Dropping a Column

ALTER TABLE employees DROP COLUMN phone_number;

Dropping a Table

The DROP TABLE statement removes a table and all its data permanently.

DROP TABLE employees;

Data Types in Oracle

Oracle provides various data types to store different kinds of data. Choosing the right data type ensures data integrity and efficient storage.

Common Data Types

Data Type	Description	Example
NUMBER(p,s)	Numeric data with precision (p) and scale (s)	NUMBER(10,2)
VARCHAR2(n)	Variable-length character string	VARCHAR2(50)
CHAR(n)	Fixed-length character string	CHAR(10)

DATE	Stores date and time	DATE
TIMESTAMP	Stores date with fractional seconds	TIMESTAMP(6)
CLOB	Large text data	CLOB
BLOB	Binary large object	BLOB

INSERT, UPDATE, DELETE Statements

Inserting Data into a Table

The INSERT INTO statement is used to add new records to a table.

Inserting a Single Row

INSERT INTO employees (employee_id, first_name, last_name, email, hire_date, salary, department_id)

VALUES (101, 'John', 'Doe', 'jdoe@example.com', SYSDATE, 5000, 10);

Inserting Multiple Rows

INSERT ALL

INTO employees (employee_id, first_name, last_name, email, hire_date, salary, department_id)

VALUES (102, 'Alice', 'Smith', 'asmith@example.com', SYSDATE, 6000, 20)

INTO employees (employee_id, first_name, last_name, email, hire_date, salary, department_id)

VALUES (103, 'Bob', 'Johnson', 'bjohnson@example.com', SYSDATE, 5500, 10)

SELECT * FROM dual;

Updating Data in a Table

The UPDATE statement modifies existing records in a table.

Updating a Single Column

UPDATE employees

SET salary = 7000

WHERE employee_id = 101;

Updating Multiple Columns

UPDATE employees

SET salary = 7500, department_id = 30

WHERE employee_id = 102;

Deleting Data from a Table

The DELETE statement removes specific records from a table.

Deleting a Single Record

DELETE FROM employees

WHERE employee_id = 103;

Deleting Multiple Records

DELETE FROM employees

WHERE department_id = 10;

Deleting All Data (Truncate vs. Delete)

The TRUNCATE TABLE statement removes all records **without logging** individual row deletions, making it faster.

TRUNCATE TABLE employees;

The DELETE statement, in contrast, logs each row deletion and allows rollback.

DELETE FROM employees;

Constraints and Indexes

Constraints in Oracle

Constraints enforce data integrity rules in tables.

Types of Constraints

Constraint	Description	Example

PRIMARY KEY	Ensures unique identification of each row	employee_id NUMBER PRIMARY KEY
UNIQUE	Ensures unique values in a column	email VARCHAR2(100) UNIQUE
NOT NULL	Prevents null values in a column	last_name VARCHAR2(50) NOT NULL
CHECK	Ensures values meet a specific condition	salary NUMBER CHECK (salary > 0)
FOREIGN KEY	Enforces referential integrity	department_id NUMBER REFERENCES departments(department_id)

Indexes in Oracle

Indexes improve query performance by allowing faster data retrieval.

Creating an Index

CREATE INDEX idx_last_name ON employees (last_name);

Creating a Unique Index

CREATE UNIQUE INDEX idx_email ON employees (email);

Dropping an Index

DROP INDEX idx_last_name;

Managing Large Data Sets

Partitioning Tables

Partitioning splits a large table into smaller, manageable pieces to enhance performance.

Example: Range Partitioning

```
CREATE TABLE sales (

    sale_id NUMBER,

    sale_date DATE,

    amount NUMBER(10,2)

)

PARTITION BY RANGE (sale_date) (

    PARTITION sales_q1 VALUES LESS THAN (TO_DATE('01-APR-2025',
'DD-MON-YYYY')),

    PARTITION sales_q2 VALUES LESS THAN (TO_DATE('01-JUL-2025',
'DD-MON-YYYY')),

    PARTITION sales_q3 VALUES LESS THAN (TO_DATE('01-OCT-2025',
'DD-MON-YYYY')),
```

PARTITION sales_q4 VALUES LESS THAN (TO_DATE('01-JAN-2026', 'DD-MON-YYYY'))

);

Bulk Data Processing

Oracle provides efficient ways to handle large amounts of data.

Using Bulk Inserts

BEGIN

   FOR i IN 1..10000 LOOP

     INSERT INTO employees (employee_id, first_name, last_name, salary, department_id)

     VALUES (i, 'Employee'||i, 'Last'||i, 5000 + i, MOD(i, 10) + 1);

   END LOOP;

   COMMIT;

END;

Using Bulk Collect for Fetching Large Data

DECLARE

   TYPE emp_table IS TABLE OF employees%ROWTYPE;

   v_employees emp_table;

BEGIN

```
    SELECT * BULK COLLECT INTO v_employees FROM employees WHERE
department_id = 10;

END;
```

Archiving Old Data

To improve performance, old data can be archived into a separate table.

```
INSERT INTO employees_archive

SELECT * FROM employees WHERE hire_date < TO_DATE('01-JAN-2015',
'DD-MON-YYYY');


DELETE FROM employees WHERE hire_date < TO_DATE('01-JAN-2015',
'DD-MON-YYYY');
```

Oracle Database Objects

Oracle Database provides various objects that enhance the functionality, efficiency, and maintainability of a database. These objects include **views, materialized views, sequences, synonyms, stored procedures, functions, triggers, and packages**. Understanding and using these objects effectively is essential for efficient database management.

Understanding Views and Materialized Views

What is a View?

A **view** is a virtual table based on a query. It does not store data itself but presents data from one or more tables. Views enhance security, simplify queries, and provide a consistent data representation.

Creating a View

A view is created using the CREATE VIEW statement.

Example: Creating a View

CREATE VIEW employee_view AS

SELECT employee_id, first_name, last_name, salary, department_id

FROM employees

WHERE salary > 5000;

This view allows users to see only employees earning more than $5000.

Using a View

You can retrieve data from a view just like a table:

SELECT * FROM employee_view;

Updating a View

If a view is based on a single table and does not contain joins, group functions, or aggregate calculations, it is **updatable**.

UPDATE employee_view

SET salary = 6000

WHERE employee_id = 101;

Dropping a View

DROP VIEW employee_view;

Materialized Views

A **materialized view** stores the results of a query physically on disk, unlike a regular view, which dynamically retrieves data from the underlying tables. Materialized views improve query performance, especially in distributed databases.

Creating a Materialized View

CREATE MATERIALIZED VIEW sales_summary

BUILD IMMEDIATE

REFRESH COMPLETE ON DEMAND

AS

SELECT department_id, SUM(salary) AS total_salary

FROM employees

GROUP BY department_id;

- **BUILD IMMEDIATE**: The materialized view is populated immediately.
- **REFRESH COMPLETE ON DEMAND**: The view is refreshed manually when needed.

Refreshing a Materialized View

EXEC DBMS_MVIEW.REFRESH('sales_summary');

Dropping a Materialized View

DROP MATERIALIZED VIEW sales_summary;

Using Sequences and Synonyms

Sequences

A **sequence** is a database object that generates unique numeric values, often used for primary key values.

Creating a Sequence

CREATE SEQUENCE emp_seq

START WITH 1

INCREMENT BY 1

NOCACHE NOCYCLE;

Using a Sequence in an INSERT Statement

INSERT INTO employees (employee_id, first_name, last_name, salary)

VALUES (emp_seq.NEXTVAL, 'John', 'Doe', 5000);

- NEXTVAL: Retrieves the next value in the sequence.
- CURRVAL: Retrieves the current value of the sequence.

Dropping a Sequence

DROP SEQUENCE emp_seq;

Synonyms

A **synonym** is an alias for a database object (such as a table, view, or procedure), simplifying access.

Creating a Synonym

CREATE SYNONYM emp FOR employees;

Now, users can use emp instead of employees:

SELECT * FROM emp;

Dropping a Synonym

DROP SYNONYM emp;

Working with Stored Procedures and Functions

Stored Procedures

A **stored procedure** is a reusable PL/SQL block that performs a specific task. It improves performance, reduces network traffic, and enhances security.

Creating a Stored Procedure

```
CREATE OR REPLACE PROCEDURE update_salary (

    p_employee_id NUMBER,

    p_salary NUMBER

) AS

BEGIN

    UPDATE employees

    SET salary = p_salary

    WHERE employee_id = p_employee_id;

    COMMIT;

END;

/
```

Executing a Stored Procedure

```
EXEC update_salary(101, 7000);
```

Dropping a Stored Procedure

DROP PROCEDURE update_salary;

Functions

A **function** returns a single value and is used in SQL statements.

Creating a Function

```
CREATE OR REPLACE FUNCTION get_employee_salary (

  p_employee_id NUMBER

) RETURN NUMBER AS

  v_salary NUMBER;

BEGIN

  SELECT salary INTO v_salary FROM employees WHERE employee_id = p_employee_id;

  RETURN v_salary;

END;

/
```

Using a Function

```
SELECT get_employee_salary(101) FROM dual;
```

Dropping a Function

DROP FUNCTION get_employee_salary;

Triggers and Their Uses

A **trigger** is a stored PL/SQL block that executes automatically in response to a database event such as an INSERT, UPDATE, or DELETE operation.

Types of Triggers

Trigger Type	Description
Before Trigger	Executes before the triggering event.
After Trigger	Executes after the triggering event.
Row-Level Trigger	Executes once for each affected row.
Statement-Level Trigger	Executes once for the entire SQL statement.

Creating a Trigger

CREATE OR REPLACE TRIGGER trg_salary_check

BEFORE INSERT OR UPDATE ON employees

FOR EACH ROW

WHEN (NEW.salary < 0)

```
BEGIN

   RAISE_APPLICATION_ERROR(-20001, 'Salary cannot be negative');

END;

/
```

This trigger prevents negative salary values.

Dropping a Trigger

```
DROP TRIGGER trg_salary_check;
```

Introduction to Packages

A **package** is a collection of related PL/SQL objects, including procedures, functions, and variables, grouped together.

Advantages of Packages

- **Encapsulation**: Groups related procedures and functions.
- **Performance**: Improves execution speed by reducing the need to recompile.
- **Security**: Grants access at the package level instead of individual procedures.

Creating a Package Specification

```
CREATE OR REPLACE PACKAGE employee_pkg AS

   PROCEDURE update_salary(p_employee_id NUMBER, p_salary NUMBER);

   FUNCTION get_salary(p_employee_id NUMBER) RETURN NUMBER;

END employee_pkg;
```

/

Creating a Package Body

```
CREATE OR REPLACE PACKAGE BODY employee_pkg AS

    PROCEDURE update_salary(p_employee_id NUMBER, p_salary NUMBER) AS

    BEGIN

        UPDATE employees SET salary = p_salary WHERE employee_id = p_employee_id;

        COMMIT;

    END update_salary;


    FUNCTION get_salary(p_employee_id NUMBER) RETURN NUMBER AS

        v_salary NUMBER;

    BEGIN

        SELECT salary INTO v_salary FROM employees WHERE employee_id = p_employee_id;

        RETURN v_salary;

    END get_salary;

END employee_pkg;
/
```

Using the Package

EXEC employee_pkg.update_salary(101, 7500);

SELECT employee_pkg.get_salary(101) FROM dual;

Dropping a Package

DROP PACKAGE employee_pkg;

PL/SQL Programming for Beginners

What is PL/SQL?

PL/SQL (Procedural Language/Structured Query Language) is Oracle's procedural extension to SQL. It enables users to write procedural code, including loops, conditionals, and exception handling, while maintaining SQL's powerful data manipulation capabilities.

Why Use PL/SQL?

- **Improved Performance:** Reduces network traffic by executing multiple SQL statements in a single block.
- **Better Security:** Encapsulates business logic and controls access through stored procedures and packages.
- **Structured Programming:** Supports variables, loops, conditionals, and exception handling.
- **Portability:** Works seamlessly with different Oracle databases.
- **Integration with SQL:** Executes SQL queries directly within procedural code.

PL/SQL Program Structure

A PL/SQL program consists of three sections:

1. **Declaration Section** – Defines variables, cursors, and types.
2. **Execution Section** – Contains procedural statements and SQL queries.
3. **Exception Handling Section** – Manages runtime errors.

Example of a Basic PL/SQL Block

```
DECLARE

  v_message VARCHAR2(50);

BEGIN

  v_message := 'Hello, PL/SQL!';

  DBMS_OUTPUT.PUT_LINE(v_message);

END;
/
```

- DECLARE – Defines variables.
- BEGIN – Starts the execution block.
- DBMS_OUTPUT.PUT_LINE – Prints output to the console.
- END – Ends the block.

Variables, Data Types, and Control Structures

Declaring Variables

PL/SQL variables must be declared before use.

Syntax

```
variable_name data_type [:= initial_value];
```

Example

```
DECLARE
```

```
    v_employee_id NUMBER := 101;

    v_employee_name VARCHAR2(50);

    v_salary NUMBER(10,2);

BEGIN

    SELECT first_name, salary INTO v_employee_name, v_salary

    FROM employees

    WHERE employee_id = v_employee_id;


    DBMS_OUTPUT.PUT_LINE('Employee: ' || v_employee_name || ' earns $' ||
v_salary);

END;

/
```

Data Types in PL/SQL

Data Type	Description
VARCHAR2(size)	Variable-length character string.
NUMBER(p,s)	Numeric data with precision p and scale s.
DATE	Stores date and time.

BOOLEAN	Stores TRUE, FALSE, or NULL.
BLOB	Stores large binary objects like images and files.

Control Structures

PL/SQL provides control structures to handle decision-making and looping.

Conditional Statements

```
DECLARE

  v_salary NUMBER := 5000;

BEGIN

  IF v_salary > 7000 THEN

    DBMS_OUTPUT.PUT_LINE('High Salary');

  ELSIF v_salary BETWEEN 5000 AND 7000 THEN

    DBMS_OUTPUT.PUT_LINE('Moderate Salary');

  ELSE

    DBMS_OUTPUT.PUT_LINE('Low Salary');

  END IF;

END;

/
```

Loops in PL/SQL

1. **Basic Loop**

```
DECLARE

    v_counter NUMBER := 1;

BEGIN

    LOOP

        DBMS_OUTPUT.PUT_LINE('Counter: ' || v_counter);

        v_counter := v_counter + 1;

        EXIT WHEN v_counter > 5;

    END LOOP;

END;

/
```

---

2. **For Loop**

```
BEGIN

    FOR i IN 1..5 LOOP

        DBMS_OUTPUT.PUT_LINE('Iteration: ' || i);

    END LOOP;

END;

/
```

---

3. **While Loop**

```
DECLARE

  v_count NUMBER := 1;

BEGIN

  WHILE v_count <= 5 LOOP

    DBMS_OUTPUT.PUT_LINE('Value: ' || v_count);

    v_count := v_count + 1;

  END LOOP;

END;

/
```

Cursors and Exception Handling

Cursors in PL/SQL

A **cursor** allows row-by-row processing of SQL query results.

Implicit Cursor (Automatic)

```
DECLARE

  v_employee_name VARCHAR2(50);

  v_salary NUMBER;

BEGIN

  SELECT first_name, salary INTO v_employee_name, v_salary

  FROM employees

  WHERE employee_id = 101;
```

```
     DBMS_OUTPUT.PUT_LINE('Employee: ' || v_employee_name || ' earns ' ||
v_salary);

END;

/
```

Explicit Cursor (Manual Control)

```
DECLARE

   CURSOR emp_cursor IS

      SELECT first_name, salary FROM employees WHERE salary > 5000;

   v_employee_name employees.first_name%TYPE;

   v_salary employees.salary%TYPE;

BEGIN

   OPEN emp_cursor;

   LOOP

      FETCH emp_cursor INTO v_employee_name, v_salary;

      EXIT WHEN emp_cursor%NOTFOUND;

      DBMS_OUTPUT.PUT_LINE(v_employee_name || ' earns ' || v_salary);

   END LOOP;

   CLOSE emp_cursor;

END;

/
```

Exception Handling

Exceptions are errors that occur during execution. PL/SQL handles them using the EXCEPTION block.

Predefined Exceptions

Exception	Cause
NO_DATA_FOUND	No rows returned by a query.
TOO_MANY_ROWS	More than one row returned when expecting one.
ZERO_DIVIDE	Division by zero.

Example

```
DECLARE
    v_salary NUMBER;
BEGIN
    SELECT salary INTO v_salary FROM employees WHERE employee_id = 9999;
EXCEPTION
    WHEN NO_DATA_FOUND THEN
        DBMS_OUTPUT.PUT_LINE('No employee found.');
```

```
WHEN TOO_MANY_ROWS THEN

    DBMS_OUTPUT.PUT_LINE('Multiple employees found.');

  WHEN OTHERS THEN

    DBMS_OUTPUT.PUT_LINE('An unexpected error occurred.');

END;

/
```

Creating and Using PL/SQL Procedures

A **procedure** is a named PL/SQL block that can be reused.

Creating a Stored Procedure

```
CREATE OR REPLACE PROCEDURE update_salary (

    p_employee_id NUMBER,

    p_new_salary NUMBER

) AS

BEGIN

    UPDATE employees SET salary = p_new_salary WHERE employee_id = p_employee_id;

    COMMIT;

    DBMS_OUTPUT.PUT_LINE('Salary updated successfully.');

END;

/
```

Executing a Procedure

EXEC update_salary(101, 7000);

Dropping a Procedure

DROP PROCEDURE update_salary;

PL/SQL Best Practices

- **Use Meaningful Variable Names:** Improve readability.
- **Use Bind Variables:** Avoid SQL injection and improve performance.
- **Handle Exceptions Properly:** Prevent runtime errors from crashing the system.
- **Minimize Cursor Usage:** Use bulk processing for large datasets.
- **Modularize Code:** Use procedures and functions for maintainability.

User Management and Security

User management and security are critical aspects of administering an Oracle database. Proper user management ensures that only authorized users have access to the database, while security policies help protect sensitive data from unauthorized access, modification, or breaches.

Oracle provides robust user authentication, authorization, and auditing mechanisms to control access and track user activities. In this chapter, we will cover:

- Creating and managing users
- Granting and revoking privileges
- Using roles and profiles for better access control
- Implementing security best practices
- Auditing and monitoring user activity

Creating and Managing Users

Oracle requires user accounts to control access to database resources. Each user is assigned specific privileges that determine what they can and cannot do.

Creating a User in Oracle

A user in Oracle is an account that can own database objects such as tables, views, and procedures. To create a user, the CREATE USER statement is used.

Syntax:

```
CREATE USER username IDENTIFIED BY password;
```

Example:

```
CREATE USER john_doe IDENTIFIED BY securePass123;
```

This creates a new user john_doe with the password securePass123.

Assigning Default Tablespace and Quotas

When creating users, it is recommended to specify a default tablespace and a temporary tablespace to prevent the user from using the SYSTEM tablespace.

```
CREATE USER john_doe

IDENTIFIED BY securePass123

DEFAULT TABLESPACE users

TEMPORARY TABLESPACE temp

QUOTA 100M ON users;
```

- DEFAULT TABLESPACE users – Assigns the users tablespace for storing objects.
- TEMPORARY TABLESPACE temp – Assigns the temp tablespace for temporary operations.
- QUOTA 100M ON users – Limits the user's storage to 100MB.

Altering a User

You can modify user attributes using the ALTER USER statement.

```
ALTER USER john_doe IDENTIFIED BY NewPass456; -- Change password
```

ALTER USER john_doe DEFAULT TABLESPACE data_ts; -- Change default tablespace

ALTER USER john_doe ACCOUNT LOCK; -- Lock the account

ALTER USER john_doe ACCOUNT UNLOCK; -- Unlock the account

Dropping a User

If a user is no longer needed, it can be removed using:

DROP USER john_doe CASCADE;

The CASCADE option ensures all objects owned by the user are also removed.

Granting and Revoking Privileges

Privileges in Oracle determine what a user can do within the database. Oracle has two types of privileges:

1. **System Privileges** – Allow users to perform administrative tasks (e.g., CREATE TABLE, CREATE USER).
2. **Object Privileges** – Allow users to perform actions on specific objects (e.g., SELECT, UPDATE, DELETE on a table).

Granting Privileges

Privileges are assigned using the GRANT statement.

Granting System Privileges

GRANT CREATE SESSION TO john_doe; -- Allows user to log in

GRANT CREATE TABLE TO john_doe; -- Allows user to create tables

GRANT UNLIMITED TABLESPACE TO john_doe; -- Allows user to use unlimited space

Granting Object Privileges

GRANT SELECT, INSERT ON employees TO john_doe;

GRANT UPDATE, DELETE ON employees TO jane_doe;

This allows john_doe to **SELECT** and **INSERT** data into the employees table, while jane_doe can **UPDATE** and **DELETE**.

Revoking Privileges

Privileges can be revoked using the REVOKE statement.

REVOKE CREATE TABLE FROM john_doe;

REVOKE SELECT, INSERT ON employees FROM john_doe;

Once revoked, the user can no longer perform these actions.

Roles and Profiles

Roles in Oracle

Roles are a collection of privileges that can be assigned to multiple users, simplifying access control.

Creating a Role

CREATE ROLE hr_manager;

Assigning Privileges to a Role

GRANT SELECT, INSERT, UPDATE, DELETE ON employees TO hr_manager;

GRANT CREATE SESSION TO hr_manager;

Assigning a Role to a User

GRANT hr_manager TO john_doe;

Now, john_doe inherits all privileges assigned to the hr_manager role.

Revoking a Role

REVOKE hr_manager FROM john_doe;

Profiles in Oracle

Profiles control user resource consumption (e.g., password policies, session limits).

Creating a Profile

CREATE PROFILE security_profile

LIMIT

   FAILED_LOGIN_ATTEMPTS 5

   PASSWORD_LIFE_TIME 90

   PASSWORD_LOCK_TIME 1;

- FAILED_LOGIN_ATTEMPTS 5 – Locks account after 5 failed login attempts.
- PASSWORD_LIFE_TIME 90 – Forces password change every 90 days.
- PASSWORD_LOCK_TIME 1 – Locks the account for 1 day after max failed attempts.

Assigning a Profile to a User

ALTER USER john_doe PROFILE security_profile;

Implementing Security Best Practices

1. **Use the Principle of Least Privilege (PoLP)** – Only grant the necessary privileges.
2. **Implement Strong Password Policies** – Require complex passwords and enforce expiration policies.
3. **Enable Account Locking** – Lock accounts after multiple failed login attempts.
4. **Use Roles Instead of Direct Privileges** – Simplifies privilege management.
5. **Encrypt Sensitive Data** – Use Oracle Transparent Data Encryption (TDE).
6. **Regularly Audit and Monitor User Activity** – Track suspicious behavior.
7. **Disable Default and Unused Accounts** – Reduce attack surface.

Auditing and Monitoring User Activity

Auditing helps track database activities, detect security violations, and maintain compliance with security policies.

Enabling Standard Auditing

AUDIT SESSION; -- Tracks user login/logout

AUDIT SELECT ON employees BY ACCESS; -- Tracks SELECT queries on employees table

```
AUDIT INSERT, UPDATE, DELETE ON employees BY ACCESS;
```

Viewing Audit Logs

```
SELECT username, action_name, timestamp

FROM dba_audit_trail

ORDER BY timestamp DESC;
```

Using Fine-Grained Auditing (FGA)

Fine-Grained Auditing allows tracking specific queries on sensitive data.

Creating an FGA Policy

```
BEGIN

  DBMS_FGA.ADD_POLICY(

    object_schema   => 'HR',

    object_name     => 'employees',

    policy_name     => 'salary_audit',

    audit_condition => 'salary > 10000',

    audit_column    => 'salary'

  );

END;

/
```

This audits queries where salary > 10000.

Monitoring Active Sessions

SELECT username, sid, serial#, status

FROM v$session

WHERE username IS NOT NULL;

Oracle Backup and Recovery

Backup and recovery are crucial aspects of Oracle database administration. A well-structured backup and recovery strategy ensures that data remains safe and available in case of hardware failures, accidental deletions, or corruption. Oracle provides various tools and methods for backing up and recovering data, ensuring minimal downtime and data loss.

In this chapter, we will explore:

- The fundamental concepts of backup and recovery
- Types of backups in Oracle
- Using Oracle Recovery Manager (RMAN)
- Performing data recovery
- Best practices for data protection

Understanding Backup and Recovery Concepts

What is Backup?

A backup is a copy of database files that can be used to restore the database in case of failure. Oracle databases consist of various file types, including:

- **Datafiles** – Store user and system data.
- **Control Files** – Contain metadata about the database.
- **Redo Log Files** – Track changes made to the database.
- **Archive Logs** – Help recover the database to a specific point in time.

What is Recovery?

Recovery is the process of restoring data from backups and applying necessary changes to bring the database to a consistent state. Oracle provides several recovery options, such as:

- **Instance Recovery** – Automatically handled by Oracle after a crash.
- **Media Recovery** – Requires restoring and applying archive logs.
- **Point-in-Time Recovery (PITR)** – Restores the database to a specific time.

Types of Oracle Backups

Oracle supports different types of backups to meet various recovery requirements.

1. Physical vs. Logical Backups

- **Physical Backups** – Copy actual database files, including datafiles, control files, and redo logs.
- **Logical Backups** – Export database objects using tools like Data Pump and EXPORT/IMPORT.

2. Full vs. Incremental Backups

- **Full Backup** – Captures the entire database, including all datafiles and control files.
- **Incremental Backup** – Captures only the changes made since the last backup, reducing storage and backup time.

3. Cold (Offline) vs. Hot (Online) Backups

- **Cold Backup** – Taken when the database is shut down, ensuring a consistent state.
- **Hot Backup** – Taken while the database is running, useful for high-availability environments.

4. Archive Log Backups

- **Archive Log Mode** enables point-in-time recovery by storing redo logs.

- **No Archive Log Mode** limits recovery options to the last full backup.

Choosing the Right Backup Type

Backup Type	Requires Database Shutdown	Supports Point-in-Time Recovery	Performance Impact
Cold Backup	Yes	No	None
Hot Backup	No	Yes	Low to Medium
Incremental Backup	No	Yes	Low

Using Recovery Manager (RMAN)

What is RMAN?

Oracle Recovery Manager (RMAN) is a built-in tool for managing database backups and recovery. It provides efficient and automated backup strategies with minimal storage requirements.

Setting Up RMAN

Start RMAN

RMAN TARGET /

1. **Check Backup Configuration**

   SHOW ALL;
2. **Performing a Full Backup**

A full database backup captures all datafiles, control files, and archive logs.

BACKUP DATABASE PLUS ARCHIVELOG;

Performing Incremental Backups

Level 0 (Equivalent to a full backup)
BACKUP INCREMENTAL LEVEL 0 DATABASE;

- **Level 1 (Captures changes since the last Level 0 or Level 1 backup)**
  BACKUP INCREMENTAL LEVEL 1 DATABASE;
- **Validating Backups**

Ensure backups are not corrupt and can be restored.

RESTORE VALIDATE DATABASE;

Performing Data Recovery

When data is lost or corrupted, different recovery techniques can be used.

1. Restoring a Full Database

If the entire database is lost, restore it using RMAN.

SHUTDOWN IMMEDIATE;

STARTUP MOUNT;

RESTORE DATABASE;

RECOVER DATABASE;

ALTER DATABASE OPEN;

---

2. Recovering a Tablespace

If a specific tablespace is corrupted or deleted:

RESTORE TABLESPACE users;

RECOVER TABLESPACE users;

ALTER DATABASE OPEN;

---

3. Recovering a Datafile

If a datafile is missing:

ALTER DATABASE DATAFILE '/oradata/users01.dbf' OFFLINE;

RESTORE DATAFILE '/oradata/users01.dbf';

RECOVER DATAFILE '/oradata/users01.dbf';

ALTER DATABASE DATAFILE '/oradata/users01.dbf' ONLINE;

---

4. Performing Point-in-Time Recovery (PITR)

To recover the database to a specific time:

RUN {

   SET UNTIL TIME "TO_DATE('2025-03-01 10:00:00', 'YYYY-MM-DD HH24:MI:SS')";

RESTORE DATABASE;

RECOVER DATABASE;

ALTER DATABASE OPEN RESETLOGS;

}

---

5. Recovering from Archived Logs

If a database crash occurs, apply archived logs:

RECOVER DATABASE USING BACKUP CONTROLFILE UNTIL CANCEL;

Best Practices for Data Protection

To ensure database reliability, follow these best practices:

1. Enable ARCHIVELOG Mode

This ensures that redo logs are archived, allowing point-in-time recovery.

SHUTDOWN IMMEDIATE;

STARTUP MOUNT;

ALTER DATABASE ARCHIVELOG;

ALTER DATABASE OPEN;

---

2. Schedule Regular Backups

Automate full and incremental backups to ensure data safety.

3. Store Backups in Multiple Locations

Maintain copies on local storage, remote servers, and cloud platforms.

4. Test Backup and Recovery Procedures

Regularly restore backups to verify their integrity.

5. Implement Data Encryption

Use Oracle Transparent Data Encryption (TDE) to secure sensitive information.

6. Monitor Backup Performance

Check backup logs to detect failures or performance issues.

SELECT * FROM V$RMAN_BACKUP_JOB_DETAILS;

---

7. Use Flashback Technologies

Flashback features allow quick recovery without restoring from backups.

Flashback Table
 FLASHBACK TABLE employees TO BEFORE DROP;

- **Flashback Database**
    FLASHBACK DATABASE TO TIMESTAMP (SYSDATE - 1);

Oracle Performance Tuning Basics

Performance tuning in Oracle is a crucial skill for database administrators (DBAs) and developers. A well-optimized database ensures high availability, efficiency, and responsiveness in handling queries and transactions. Oracle provides various tools and techniques to optimize database performance, minimize bottlenecks, and enhance system efficiency.

In this chapter, we will explore:

- Understanding database performance issues
- Optimizing SQL queries
- Using **EXPLAIN PLAN** and indexing
- Monitoring system performance
- Basic troubleshooting techniques

Understanding Database Performance Issues

What is Performance Tuning?

Performance tuning involves identifying bottlenecks and optimizing database processes to enhance performance. This includes improving SQL queries, indexing, memory usage, and system resources.

Common Database Performance Issues

Performance problems in Oracle databases can arise from multiple factors. Here are some of the most common issues:

1. **Slow Queries**

   ○ Poorly written SQL queries
   ○ Missing or inefficient indexes
   ○ Excessive table joins and complex subqueries

2. **High CPU and Memory Usage**

   ○ Poor memory allocation for processes
   ○ Insufficient database caching
   ○ Unoptimized queries consuming excessive CPU

3. **Disk I/O Bottlenecks**

   ○ High read/write operations on storage
   ○ Fragmented tables and indexes
   ○ Insufficient disk space for tablespace growth

4. **Locking and Contention Issues**

   ○ Excessive row locking causing transaction delays
   ○ Deadlocks between multiple transactions
   ○ Poor concurrency management

5. **Slow Database Connections**

   ○ High session contention
   ○ Overloaded listener and networking issues

Key Metrics for Performance Monitoring

Oracle provides performance metrics to analyze database efficiency:

Metric	Description
CPU Usage	High CPU consumption affects query processing speed.

Memory Usage	Poor memory allocation can slow down transactions.
Disk I/O	High read/write latency can cause performance issues.
Wait Events	Indicates bottlenecks in query execution.
Buffer Cache Hit Ratio	Measures how efficiently the database is utilizing memory cache.

Optimizing SQL Queries

SQL optimization is one of the most effective ways to improve database performance. A well-structured SQL query can reduce CPU usage, memory consumption, and query execution time.

1. Writing Efficient SQL Queries

Use SELECT Only What You Need

Instead of selecting all columns, retrieve only required columns.

```
-- Inefficient

SELECT * FROM employees;


-- Optimized
```

SELECT first_name, last_name, department_id FROM employees;

Use EXISTS Instead of IN for Subqueries

The EXISTS operator is more efficient than IN when checking existence in large datasets.

-- Less Efficient

SELECT first_name FROM employees WHERE department_id IN (SELECT department_id FROM departments WHERE location_id = 1700);

-- Optimized

SELECT first_name FROM employees WHERE EXISTS (SELECT 1 FROM departments WHERE employees.department_id = departments.department_id AND location_id = 1700);

Use Joins Instead of Subqueries

Joins are generally more efficient than correlated subqueries.

-- Less Efficient

SELECT e.first_name, d.department_name

FROM employees e

WHERE department_id = (SELECT department_id FROM departments WHERE department_name = 'Sales');

-- Optimized

```
SELECT e.first_name, d.department_name

FROM employees e

JOIN departments d ON e.department_id = d.department_id

WHERE d.department_name = 'Sales';
```

Use Bind Variables

Bind variables improve query execution time by reducing parsing overhead.

```
-- Inefficient

SELECT * FROM employees WHERE employee_id = 101;
```

```
-- Optimized (Using Bind Variable)

SELECT * FROM employees WHERE employee_id = :emp_id;
```

Using EXPLAIN PLAN and Indexing

1. Using EXPLAIN PLAN

The EXPLAIN PLAN command provides execution details on how Oracle processes a SQL query.

Generating an Execution Plan

```
EXPLAIN PLAN FOR

SELECT first_name FROM employees WHERE department_id = 50;
```

```
SELECT * FROM TABLE(DBMS_XPLAN.DISPLAY);
```

This output shows whether the query is using full table scans, indexes, or joins.

Interpreting the Execution Plan

Operation	Description
TABLE ACCESS FULL	Full table scan (inefficient for large tables).
INDEX SCAN	Optimized index-based lookup.
HASH JOIN	Used for joining large tables efficiently.
SORT ORDER BY	Sorting operation, can be costly if not indexed.

2. Using Indexing for Performance Improvement

Indexes improve query performance by speeding up data retrieval.

Types of Indexes

Index Type	Description
B-tree Index	Default index type, good for most queries.

Bitmap Index	Useful for low-cardinality columns (e.g., Gender: M/F).
Function-Based Index	Indexes expressions or computed values.
Partitioned Index	Improves performance for large datasets by dividing data into partitions.

Creating an Index

CREATE INDEX emp_dept_idx ON employees(department_id);

Using Function-Based Index

If a query involves a function on a column, an index can be created for faster retrieval.

CREATE INDEX emp_lower_idx ON employees(LOWER(last_name));

Checking Index Usage

SELECT index_name, table_name, uniqueness FROM user_indexes WHERE table_name = 'EMPLOYEES';

Monitoring System Performance

Oracle provides built-in views and tools for monitoring performance.

1. Using V$ Views for Performance Analysis

View	Purpose
V$SESSION	Shows current user sessions.
V$SQLAREA	Provides SQL execution statistics.
V$SYSTEM_EVENT	Displays wait events affecting performance.
V$SESSION_WAIT	Shows active session wait states.

Checking Active Sessions

SELECT sid, serial#, username, status FROM v$session;

Identifying Slow Queries

SELECT sql_text, executions, elapsed_time

FROM v$sql

ORDER BY elapsed_time DESC FETCH FIRST 10 ROWS ONLY;

Checking Wait Events

SELECT event, total_waits FROM v$system_event ORDER BY total_waits DESC;

Basic Troubleshooting Techniques

When performance issues arise, follow these troubleshooting steps:

1. Identify High CPU Usage Queries

```
SELECT sql_id, sql_text, cpu_time FROM v$sql ORDER BY cpu_time DESC
FETCH FIRST 5 ROWS ONLY;
```

2. Fix Full Table Scans

If TABLE ACCESS FULL appears in the execution plan, check if an index can be used.

3. Analyze Locking Issues

```
SELECT blocking_session, sid, serial#, wait_class, seconds_in_wait

FROM v$session WHERE blocking_session IS NOT NULL;
```

4. Tune Database Memory

Ensure that the **SGA (System Global Area)** and **PGA (Program Global Area)** are properly allocated:

```
SHOW PARAMETER sga_target;

SHOW PARAMETER pga_aggregate_target;
```

5. Rebuild Indexes if Fragmented

```
ALTER INDEX emp_dept_idx REBUILD;
```

Working with Oracle Cloud Database

Oracle Cloud Database offers a scalable, secure, and high-performance environment for managing databases in the cloud. It provides various deployment models, including Autonomous Database, Bare Metal, Virtual Machine, and Exadata, allowing businesses to leverage cloud capabilities while reducing on-premises infrastructure costs.

In this chapter, we will explore:

- **Introduction to Oracle Cloud Infrastructure**
- **Deploying and Managing Oracle Databases in the Cloud**
- **Cloud Security and Best Practices**
- **Backup and Disaster Recovery in the Cloud**
- **Oracle Autonomous Database**

Introduction to Oracle Cloud Infrastructure (OCI)

Oracle Cloud Infrastructure (OCI) is Oracle's cloud computing platform designed to provide secure, scalable, and high-performance computing resources. It supports various cloud services, including compute, networking, storage, and database solutions.

Key Features of Oracle Cloud Infrastructure

- **High Performance** – OCI offers low-latency networking and high-speed storage for enterprise-grade workloads.

- **Scalability** – Supports horizontal and vertical scaling to handle growing business needs.
- **Security** – Built-in security features such as identity and access management (IAM), encryption, and threat detection.
- **Global Reach** – Multiple data centers worldwide for optimized performance and compliance.
- **Cost-Effective** – Flexible pricing models, including pay-as-you-go and reserved instances.

Oracle Database Deployment Options in OCI

Deployment Option	Description
Bare Metal Database	High-performance dedicated servers for maximum control and security.
Virtual Machine (VM) Database	Cost-effective and scalable database deployment.
Exadata Cloud Service	High-performance Exadata technology in the cloud.
Autonomous Database	Fully managed, self-driving database with AI-driven automation.

Deploying and Managing Oracle Databases in the Cloud

Oracle Cloud provides multiple ways to deploy and manage databases. The deployment process involves creating a database instance, configuring network settings, and ensuring security measures are in place.

Steps to Deploy an Oracle Database in OCI

1. **Log in to Oracle Cloud Console**
   ○ Navigate to cloud.oracle.com and sign in.
2. **Select Database Service**
   ○ Choose the appropriate database type: Bare Metal, VM, Exadata, or Autonomous Database.
3. **Configure Database Details**
   ○ Choose database edition, compute size, and storage capacity.
   ○ Set administrative credentials (e.g., SYS, SYSTEM passwords).
4. **Networking Configuration**
   ○ Define Virtual Cloud Network (VCN) and Subnet for connectivity.
   ○ Enable Public or Private Access as needed.
5. **Create and Launch the Database**
   ○ Click "Create" and wait for the database to be provisioned.
6. **Access and Manage the Database**
   ○ Use **SQL Developer**, **SSH**, or **SQL*Plus** to connect and manage the database.

Managing Oracle Cloud Databases

Once deployed, databases require ongoing management, including performance tuning, backup configuration, and monitoring.

Task	Tool/Method
Monitor Performance	Oracle Cloud Console, OCI Monitoring

Apply Patches & Updates	Automatic patching or manual updates
Scale Resources	Increase CPU, memory, or storage as needed
Configure High Availability	Use Data Guard for failover protection

---

Cloud Security and Best Practices

Security is a critical aspect of managing Oracle databases in the cloud. OCI provides built-in security features to protect databases against unauthorized access, breaches, and cyber threats.

Key Security Features in OCI

1. **Identity and Access Management (IAM)**

   o Create and manage users, groups, and roles.
   o Assign least-privilege policies for secure access.

2. **Data Encryption**

   o Encrypt data at rest using Transparent Data Encryption (TDE).
   o Use Oracle-managed or customer-managed keys in **OCI Vault**.

3. **Network Security**

   o Use **Virtual Cloud Networks (VCNs)** with private subnets.
   o Configure **Security Lists** and **Network Security Groups (NSGs)** for traffic control.

4. **Auditing and Monitoring**

- ○ Enable **Oracle Cloud Guard** for proactive threat detection.
- ○ Use **Oracle Audit Vault** for compliance monitoring.

Best Practices for Cloud Security

- **Use Multi-Factor Authentication (MFA)** for enhanced login security.
- **Apply Patches and Updates** regularly to fix vulnerabilities.
- **Restrict Public Access** to minimize exposure to unauthorized users.
- **Use Private Endpoints** for secure database connections.

Backup and Disaster Recovery in the Cloud

Oracle Cloud provides robust backup and disaster recovery solutions to ensure data availability and business continuity.

Types of Backups in Oracle Cloud

Backup Type	Description
Full Backup	Backs up the entire database, including system and user data.
Incremental Backup	Backs up only changes since the last backup, reducing storage costs.
RMAN Backup	Uses Oracle Recovery Manager (RMAN) for automated, efficient backups.

| **Automatic Backups** | Enables scheduled backups for Autonomous Database. |

Configuring Automatic Backups

1. Navigate to **Database Details** in Oracle Cloud Console.
2. Enable **Automatic Backups** under Backup Settings.
3. Specify retention period (7 to 60 days).
4. Store backups in **OCI Object Storage**.

Disaster Recovery Solutions

1. **Oracle Data Guard**

   o Provides real-time replication for high availability.
   o Configures primary and standby databases.

2. **Oracle GoldenGate**

   o Enables data replication across different cloud regions.
   o Supports near-zero downtime migrations.

3. **Cross-Region Backups**

   o Store backups in a secondary region for additional protection.

Oracle Autonomous Database

Oracle Autonomous Database is a self-managing, self-patching, and self-tuning database that leverages machine learning (ML) and automation.

Key Features of Oracle Autonomous Database

- **Automated Performance Tuning** – AI-based SQL optimization.
- **Automatic Scaling** – Dynamically adjusts resources based on workload.

- **Self-Healing** – Detects and resolves failures automatically.
- **Built-in Security** – Continuous encryption and security monitoring.

Types of Autonomous Databases

Database Type	Use Case
Autonomous Transaction Processing (ATP)	Optimized for OLTP workloads.
Autonomous Data Warehouse (ADW)	Designed for analytics and reporting.
Autonomous JSON Database	Specialized for JSON-based applications.
Autonomous Graph Database	Used for managing graph data relationships.

Deploying an Autonomous Database

1. **Go to OCI Console** → Select "Autonomous Database."
2. **Choose Database Type** (ATP or ADW).
3. **Configure Compute & Storage** (CPU cores, storage size).
4. **Set Admin Password** for database access.
5. **Enable Auto-Scaling** for resource flexibility.
6. **Launch the Database** and connect using **SQL Developer** or **JDBC/ODBC**.

Managing an Autonomous Database

- Monitor database performance using **OCI Monitoring**.

- Configure auto-scaling for cost-efficient operations.
- Use built-in **AI-driven analytics** for workload optimization.

Real-World Applications of Oracle

Oracle Database is one of the most widely used database management systems (DBMS) in the world, supporting mission-critical applications across industries such as finance, healthcare, retail, telecommunications, and government. Its robust features, scalability, and security make it a preferred choice for businesses of all sizes.

This chapter explores:

- **Using Oracle in Enterprise Applications**
- **Oracle for Business Intelligence and Data Warehousing**
- **Oracle and Big Data Integration**
- **Case Studies and Industry Examples**
- **Learning Paths for Oracle Certification**

Using Oracle in Enterprise Applications

Enterprise applications require a database solution that is scalable, secure, and high-performing. Oracle Database meets these requirements, offering a range of solutions for business applications, customer relationship management (CRM), enterprise resource planning (ERP), and supply chain management (SCM).

Key Features of Oracle for Enterprises

1. **High Availability & Scalability** – Oracle Real Application Clusters (RAC) provide continuous availability and horizontal scaling.

2. **Security & Compliance** – Advanced security features such as Transparent Data Encryption (TDE) and Data Masking.
3. **Data Integrity & Consistency** – ACID-compliant transactions ensure reliable and consistent data.
4. **Multi-Model Database** – Supports relational, JSON, XML, and graph data for diverse applications.
5. **Performance Optimization** – Advanced indexing, caching, and partitioning for high-speed queries.

Common Enterprise Use Cases

Application Type	Oracle Database Usage
Customer Relationship Management (CRM)	Stores customer data, interactions, and analytics for sales and marketing teams.
Enterprise Resource Planning (ERP)	Manages finance, HR, supply chain, and operations in a single database.
Supply Chain Management (SCM)	Tracks inventory, logistics, and vendor data with real-time reporting.
Human Capital Management (HCM)	Stores employee records, payroll, and performance data securely.
E-commerce & Online Transactions	Ensures fast, secure, and scalable online payment and order processing.

Oracle for Business Intelligence and Data Warehousing

Oracle Database plays a critical role in business intelligence (BI) and data warehousing by helping organizations transform raw data into actionable insights.

What is Business Intelligence (BI)?

Business Intelligence refers to technologies and strategies used to analyze business data and support decision-making. Oracle provides tools like **Oracle Analytics Cloud (OAC)** and **Oracle BI Enterprise Edition (OBIEE)** to facilitate data-driven insights.

Oracle Data Warehousing Solutions

Oracle offers specialized tools for managing large-scale data warehouses:

1. **Oracle Exadata** – Optimized for high-speed data processing and analytics.
2. **Oracle Autonomous Data Warehouse (ADW)** – A self-managing, cloud-based data warehouse solution.
3. **Oracle Big Data SQL** – Allows seamless querying of structured and unstructured data.
4. **Oracle OLAP (Online Analytical Processing)** – Enables complex analytical queries and multidimensional data modeling.

Business Intelligence Workflow with Oracle

1. **Data Collection** – Extracting data from multiple sources (ERP, CRM, IoT, social media).
2. **Data Integration** – Using **Oracle Data Integrator (ODI)** to clean and transform data.
3. **Data Storage** – Storing data in **Oracle Data Warehouse** or **Exadata**.
4. **Data Analysis** – Running queries using **SQL, PL/SQL, and Oracle BI tools**.
5. **Visualization & Reporting** – Generating dashboards and reports with **Oracle Analytics Cloud**.

Industries Using Oracle for BI

Industry	BI Applications
Retail	Customer segmentation, demand forecasting, and trend analysis.
Finance	Fraud detection, risk analysis, and financial reporting.
Healthcare	Patient data analytics, treatment outcomes, and hospital performance metrics.
Manufacturing	Supply chain optimization and predictive maintenance.
Telecommunications	Customer churn analysis and network performance monitoring.

Oracle and Big Data Integration

In the era of big data, organizations generate vast amounts of structured and unstructured data from multiple sources. Oracle provides solutions to store, process, and analyze this data effectively.

How Oracle Integrates with Big Data

1. **Oracle Big Data SQL** – Enables SQL queries across Hadoop, NoSQL, and Oracle Databases.

2. **Oracle Big Data Appliance** – A pre-configured, high-performance hardware/software solution for big data processing.
3. **Oracle Data Lakehouse** – Combines the scalability of a data lake with the structure of a data warehouse.
4. **Oracle Autonomous Data Warehouse** – Uses AI-driven automation for managing big data workloads.

Oracle Technologies for Big Data

Technology	Function
Oracle NoSQL Database	Handles unstructured data at massive scale.
Oracle GoldenGate	Real-time data replication for big data streaming.
Oracle Data Integrator (ODI)	ETL (Extract, Transform, Load) for big data pipelines.
Oracle Stream Analytics	Analyzes real-time data streams for event processing.

Big Data Use Cases with Oracle

- **Financial Fraud Detection** – Analyzing transaction patterns to prevent fraud.
- **Predictive Maintenance** – Using sensor data in manufacturing to predict equipment failures.
- **Personalized Marketing** – Leveraging big data analytics for targeted advertising.

- **Healthcare Research** – Processing genomic data for personalized medicine.

Case Studies and Industry Examples

1. Banking and Finance – JPMorgan Chase

Challenge: Needed a secure, scalable, and high-performance database for financial transactions.
Solution: Used Oracle Exadata and Oracle RAC to handle millions of transactions daily.
Result: Improved transaction processing speed and fraud detection capabilities.

2. Retail – Walmart

Challenge: Managing massive customer transaction data for inventory and sales forecasting.
Solution: Implemented Oracle Data Warehouse and BI tools.
Result: Optimized inventory management, reducing stock shortages and excesses.

3. Healthcare – Mayo Clinic

Challenge: Processing large volumes of patient records while ensuring data security.
Solution: Used Oracle Autonomous Database with AI-driven analytics.
Result: Improved patient care, faster diagnostics, and compliance with healthcare regulations.

4. Telecommunications – AT&T

Challenge: Managing massive call records and network data for performance monitoring.
Solution: Deployed Oracle Big Data solutions and Oracle Stream Analytics.
Result: Optimized network performance and reduced customer churn.

Learning Paths for Oracle Certification

For individuals looking to advance their careers in Oracle Database administration, development, or cloud computing, Oracle offers various certification programs.

Popular Oracle Certifications

Certification	Description
Oracle Certified Associate (OCA)	Entry-level certification for database fundamentals.
Oracle Certified Professional (OCP)	Advanced skills in database administration and performance tuning.
Oracle Certified Expert (OCE)	Specialization in specific areas like RAC, security, or SQL tuning.
Oracle Cloud Infrastructure (OCI) Certifications	Focuses on Oracle Cloud Database services.

Steps to Get Certified

1. Choose a certification path (Database, Developer, Cloud, etc.).
2. Study official Oracle materials, books, and online courses.
3. Gain hands-on experience using Oracle Cloud Free Tier or local installations.
4. Practice with exam simulators and sample questions.
5. Register for the certification exam through **Oracle University**.

Resources and Next Steps

As you conclude your journey through this book, it's essential to have access to the right resources to continue your learning and apply your knowledge effectively. The world of Oracle Database is vast and constantly evolving, and staying up to date with the latest trends, tools, and best practices will help you become a proficient Oracle professional.

This chapter will provide:

- **Recommended Books and Online Courses**
- **Oracle Certification Paths**
- **Oracle Community and Support Forums**
- **Keeping Up with Oracle Updates**
- **Final Thoughts and Best Practices**

Recommended Books and Online Courses

Books for Further Learning

There are many excellent books available for those looking to deepen their understanding of Oracle Database and related technologies. Below are some highly recommended ones:

Book Title	Author(s)	Description

Oracle Database 19c: The Complete Reference	Kevin Loney	A comprehensive guide covering all aspects of Oracle 19c, from basic to advanced concepts.
Oracle PL/SQL Programming	Steven Feuerstein	A detailed book focused on PL/SQL programming, ideal for those who want to master procedural programming in Oracle.
Oracle Database Administration for Absolute Beginners	Darl Kuhn	A beginner-friendly guide to Oracle database administration concepts.
Oracle Performance Tuning Guide	Rich Niemiec	A detailed book on optimizing and tuning Oracle databases for performance.
Oracle Big Data Handbook	Tom Plunkett	A practical guide on using Oracle for big data analytics and data warehousing.

Online Courses and Training

Many platforms offer high-quality Oracle training, both free and paid. Below are some recommended platforms:

1. **Oracle University** (https://education.oracle.com/) – Official training and certification programs from Oracle.
2. **Udemy** (https://www.udemy.com/) – Offers a variety of Oracle courses, including SQL, PL/SQL, and Oracle Database Administration.
3. **Coursera** (https://www.coursera.org/) – Features Oracle courses from universities and industry experts.
4. **LinkedIn Learning** (https://www.linkedin.com/learning/) – Offers professional Oracle training courses for different expertise levels.
5. **Pluralsight** (https://www.pluralsight.com/) – High-quality video courses on Oracle administration, development, and security.

Oracle Certification Paths

Oracle certifications validate your expertise and help you stand out in the job market. Whether you are an aspiring Oracle developer, database administrator, or cloud architect, earning an Oracle certification can open doors to career growth.

Popular Oracle Certifications and Paths

Certification	Description	Best For
Oracle Certified Foundations Associate (OCFA)	Entry-level certification for beginners covering basic database and cloud concepts.	Students, Beginners
Oracle Certified Associate (OCA)	Covers SQL, PL/SQL, and database administration fundamentals.	Junior Developers, DBAs

Oracle Certified Professional (OCP)	Intermediate-level certification for managing and tuning databases.	Mid-level DBAs, Developers
Oracle Certified Expert (OCE)	Specializations in areas like performance tuning, security, and RAC.	Experienced DBAs, Specialists
Oracle Cloud Infrastructure (OCI) Architect Associate	Validates knowledge of Oracle Cloud services and deployment strategies.	Cloud Engineers, Architects
Oracle Cloud Infrastructure (OCI) Architect Professional	Advanced cloud certification for designing complex Oracle Cloud solutions.	Senior Cloud Engineers

Steps to Get Certified

1. **Choose the Right Certification Path** – Select a certification based on your career goals.
2. **Prepare with Official Training** – Use Oracle University, books, and online courses.
3. **Gain Hands-On Experience** – Set up a test environment using Oracle Free Tier or VirtualBox.
4. **Take Practice Exams** – Utilize practice questions and mock tests.
5. **Schedule and Pass the Exam** – Register through **Pearson VUE** (Oracle's official testing partner).

Oracle Community and Support Forums

Learning from experts and engaging with the Oracle community is a great way to accelerate your growth. Oracle has an active global community where you can ask questions, share knowledge, and stay informed about the latest developments.

Official Oracle Communities

- **Oracle Community** (https://community.oracle.com/) – A forum where Oracle users discuss best practices, troubleshooting, and new technologies.
- **Oracle Developer Community** (https://developer.oracle.com/) – A platform for Oracle developers to collaborate and share resources.
- **Oracle GitHub Repository** (https://github.com/oracle) – Open-source projects and tools from Oracle.

Popular Online Forums and Groups

- **Stack Overflow** (https://stackoverflow.com/) – Get help on Oracle-related programming and database queries.
- **Reddit – r/oracle** (https://www.reddit.com/r/oracle/) – A community for Oracle professionals and enthusiasts.
- **LinkedIn Oracle Groups** – Join professional groups dedicated to Oracle database technologies.

Oracle Conferences and Events

Attending Oracle conferences can help you network with industry professionals and stay updated with the latest innovations. Some key events include:

- **Oracle CloudWorld** – Oracle's annual flagship conference covering cloud computing and database innovations.
- **Oracle Developer Live** – Free virtual sessions covering Oracle technologies.
- **Oracle OpenWorld** – A premier event showcasing Oracle's latest technologies and strategies.

Keeping Up with Oracle Updates

Oracle continually releases updates, security patches, and new features. Staying informed about these changes is essential for database administrators, developers, and IT professionals.

Ways to Stay Updated

1. **Follow Oracle Blogs** (https://blogs.oracle.com/) – Get the latest announcements, tutorials, and industry insights.
2. **Subscribe to Oracle Newsletters** – Receive updates on new features and security alerts.
3. **Monitor Oracle Support Notes (MOS)** – Access My Oracle Support (MOS) for critical security patches and bug fixes.
4. **Engage in Oracle Webinars** – Attend online webinars for live demonstrations and training.
5. **Follow Oracle on Social Media** – Stay connected via Twitter (@oracle), LinkedIn, and YouTube.

Final Thoughts and Best Practices

Mastering Oracle Database is a rewarding journey that requires continuous learning and practical application. Here are some key best practices to follow:

1. Build a Strong Foundation

- Start with SQL and PL/SQL before diving into advanced administration topics.
- Understand Oracle's architecture and how databases operate internally.

2. Practice with Real-World Scenarios

- Set up a test environment using **Oracle Free Tier** or **Oracle VirtualBox**.

- Work on sample projects, such as building a small database application.

3. Follow Security Best Practices

- Always use **least privilege principles** when granting user access.
- Implement **data encryption** and **regular backups**.

4. Optimize for Performance

- Learn how to use **EXPLAIN PLAN** and **SQL Tuning Advisor**.
- Use **indexing** and **partitioning** effectively.

5. Stay Curious and Keep Learning

- Explore new Oracle technologies such as **Autonomous Database** and **Oracle Cloud Infrastructure**.
- Keep track of Oracle certification updates and industry trends.

This book has provided a beginner-friendly yet comprehensive guide to Oracle Database, covering everything from installation and SQL fundamentals to cloud deployment and performance tuning.

Your journey doesn't end here. By leveraging the right resources, pursuing Oracle certifications, engaging with the community, and staying updated with new developments, you can build a successful career as an Oracle professional.

What's Next?

- **Start a hands-on project** to apply what you've learned.
- **Join an Oracle user group** to network with other professionals.
- **Prepare for an Oracle certification** to validate your skills.
- **Continue exploring Oracle Cloud** to stay ahead in the evolving tech landscape.

With dedication and continuous learning, you'll soon become proficient in Oracle Database and open doors to exciting career opportunities in database administration, development, and cloud computing.

Glossary of Terms

A

- **ACID (Atomicity, Consistency, Isolation, Durability)** – A set of properties that ensure reliable database transactions.
- **Aggregate Functions** – SQL functions that perform calculations on multiple rows, such as SUM(), AVG(), COUNT(), MIN(), and MAX().
- **Alias** – A temporary name assigned to a table or column in SQL queries using the AS keyword.
- **ALTER** – A SQL command used to modify an existing database object, such as a table or column.
- **Analytic Functions** – Advanced SQL functions (e.g., RANK(), DENSE_RANK(), LAG(), LEAD()) used for complex calculations over result sets.
- **ANSI SQL** – The standardized version of SQL defined by the American National Standards Institute (ANSI).
- **Authentication** – The process of verifying the identity of a user or system accessing a database.
- **Autonomous Database** – A self-managing Oracle Cloud database that automates tuning, backups, and security.

B

- **Backup** – A copy of database data used for recovery in case of failure or corruption.

- **BLOB (Binary Large Object)** – A data type used to store large binary data, such as images and multimedia files.
- **Blocking Session** – A database session that holds a lock on a resource, preventing other sessions from accessing it.
- **Bridge Table** – A table used in a many-to-many relationship to link two tables together.
- **Buffer Cache** – A memory area where frequently accessed data blocks are stored to improve performance.

C

- **Cartesian Join** – A type of join that returns the Cartesian product of two tables, resulting in every row from the first table being combined with every row from the second table.
- **CHAR vs. VARCHAR** – CHAR is a fixed-length string data type, while VARCHAR is a variable-length string data type.
- **Check Constraint** – A constraint used to enforce domain integrity by limiting the values allowed in a column.
- **Clustered Index** – A type of index that determines the physical order of data rows in a table.
- **Cold Backup** – A database backup taken while the database is offline.
- **Commit** – A SQL command that saves all changes made by a transaction.
- **Concurrency** – The ability of a database to handle multiple transactions simultaneously without conflicts.
- **Cursor** – A database object used to retrieve and process multiple rows one at a time in PL/SQL.

D

- **Data Dictionary** – A collection of metadata tables that store information about database objects such as tables, indexes, and users.

- **Data Guard** – An Oracle feature that provides high availability, disaster recovery, and data protection by maintaining standby databases.
- **Database Link** – A connection that allows one Oracle database to communicate with another remote database.
- **DDL (Data Definition Language)** – SQL commands (CREATE, ALTER, DROP, TRUNCATE) used to define and modify database structures.
- **DML (Data Manipulation Language)** – SQL commands (SELECT, INSERT, UPDATE, DELETE) used to manipulate data within tables.
- **Deadlock** – A situation where two or more database transactions are waiting for each other to release locks, preventing progress.
- **Denormalization** – The process of combining normalized tables to improve performance, often at the cost of data redundancy.
- **Dynamic SQL** – SQL statements that are constructed and executed at runtime instead of being precompiled.

E

- **Entity Relationship Diagram (ERD)** – A visual representation of database tables and their relationships.
- **Escalation (Lock Escalation)** – The process where fine-grained row or page locks are converted into coarser table-level locks.
- **Explain Plan** – A SQL tool that shows the execution path of a query, helping with performance tuning.
- **Export/Import** – Oracle utilities (expdp/impdp) used for exporting and importing database objects and data.
- **Extent** – A contiguous block of storage allocated to a database object like a table or index.

F

- **Flashback** – An Oracle feature that allows recovering data from past states without restoring from backups.

- **Foreign Key** – A column or set of columns in one table that establishes a relationship with the primary key of another table.
- **Full Table Scan** – A method of retrieving data by scanning an entire table instead of using an index.

G

- **GRANT** – A SQL command used to provide users with specific privileges.
- **Global Temporary Table** – A table that holds session-specific data and is automatically dropped when the session ends.

H

- **Hash Join** – A join algorithm that uses hash tables to improve performance when joining large tables.
- **Heap Table** – A standard table in Oracle that does not use indexes for data organization.
- **High Availability** – Techniques used to ensure minimal downtime of database services, such as clustering and replication.

I

- **Index** – A database object that speeds up data retrieval by creating a lookup structure.
- **INNER JOIN** – A join that retrieves only matching rows from the related tables.
- **INSERT** – A SQL command used to add new records to a table.
- **Isolation Levels** – Different levels of transaction isolation (READ COMMITTED, SERIALIZABLE, etc.) that control how concurrent transactions interact.

J

- **JOIN** – A SQL operation used to combine rows from two or more tables based on a related column.
- **JSON (JavaScript Object Notation)** – A lightweight data format that can be stored and queried in Oracle databases.

K

- **Key Constraint** – A database constraint that enforces uniqueness and referential integrity (e.g., PRIMARY KEY, FOREIGN KEY).
- **Kill Session** – The process of terminating a running database session to free up resources.

L

- **Locking Mechanism** – A feature that controls concurrent access to database resources.
- **LOB (Large Object)** – A data type used to store large text (CLOB) and binary (BLOB) data.

M

- **Materialized View** – A database object that stores query results for faster retrieval.
- **Metadata** – Data that describes database structures, such as table definitions and index properties.

N

- **Normalization** – The process of organizing a database to reduce redundancy and improve integrity.
- **NoSQL** – A non-relational database model used for handling large-scale, unstructured data.

O

- **Optimizer** – A database component that determines the most efficient way to execute a SQL query.
- **Oracle Net Services** – A suite of tools that manage communication between Oracle databases and clients.

P

- **Partitioning** – A technique used to divide large tables into smaller, more manageable pieces for improved performance.
- **PL/SQL** – A procedural extension of SQL used for writing stored procedures, triggers, and functions.

R

- **RAC (Real Application Clusters)** – An Oracle feature that allows multiple instances to run on different servers, sharing a single database.
- **Rollback** – A SQL command used to undo uncommitted transactions.

S-Z

- **Schema** – A collection of database objects owned by a user.
- **Sequence** – A database object that generates unique numbers.

- **Trigger** – A PL/SQL block that executes automatically when certain events occur.
- **View** – A virtual table based on the result of a SQL query.
- **XML DB** – Oracle's native support for XML storage and querying.

www.ingramcontent.com/pod-product-compliance
Lightning Source LLC
LaVergne TN
LVHW081700050326
832903LV00026B/1839